ABERDEEN REMEMBERED

by
Aberdeen City Libraries and Museums

These youngsters are seated beside the railings at the corner of St Nicholas Street and Union Street near the statue of Queen Victoria – a busy area that must have made an excellent site for attracting prospective customers. 'I'll meet you at the Queen' was one of the local sayings until the statue was moved to Queen's Cross in 1964. One of the lads is barefoot. The beautifully crafted railings were removed when the pavement was widened in 1965 in conjunction with the expansion of the nearby Marks & Spencer store.

© Aberdeen City Libraries and Museums 2003
First published in the United Kingdom, 2003,
by Stenlake Publishing
Printed by Cordfall Ltd., Glasgow G21 2QA

ISBN 1 84033 268 9

FURTHER READING

All of these books are available for consultation in the Reference and Local Studies Department of Aberdeen Central Library. Please note that none are available from Stenlake Publishing.

Dennison, E. Patricia; Ditchburn, David; Lynch, Michael, editors, *Aberdeen Before 1800: A New History*, 2002

Fraser, W. Hamish & Lee, Clive H., editors, *Aberdeen 1800–2000: A New History*, 2000

Mackenzie, Hugh, *Third Statistical Account of Scotland*, City of Aberdeen, 1953

Keith, Alexander, *A Thousand Years of Aberdeen*, 1972

Meldrum, Edward, *Aberdeen of Old*, 1986

Anderson, Robert, *Aberdeen in Byegone Days: Views of Streets and Buildings*, 1910

Fraser, G. M., *Aberdeen Street Names; Their History, Meaning, and Personal Associations*, (1911); with new foreword and supplement by Moira Henderson, 1986

Clark, Victoria E., *Port of Aberdeen: A History of its Trade and Shipping From the 12th Century to the Present Day*, 1921

Turner, John R., *Scotland's North Sea Gateway: Aberdeen Harbour, AD 1136–1986*, 1986

Aberdeen Today: A Record of the Life, Thought, and Industry of the City, 1907

ACKNOWLEDGEMENTS

The photographs in this publication have been selected from the collections held in Aberdeen City Libraries and Museums. The library staff gratefully acknowledge the photographic services and enthusiasm of David Clark of Laurencekirk.

The premises of G. D. Henderson, plumber and ironmonger, at 23 Bon-Accord Terrace. Garnet Henderson was the son of a granite polisher and appears for the first time in the *Aberdeen Directory* of 1910/11, remaining in business until 1966/67. Both he and his brother William, who worked with him, were regular winners of athletic events at Highland games in the north-east, excelling in sprints and high jump. The advert above the door reading 'Veritas Mantles are the best' recalls the days when gas lighting was the norm and these fragile mantles were needed to illuminate the home.

INTRODUCTION

Aberdeen's location between the Rivers Dee and Don meant that for many centuries the city's prosperity was closely linked with the development of its harbour, which until relatively recently provided the easiest access point. The construction of new roads in the 1800s and the arrival of the railway in 1850 offered alternative routes into the city, but the harbour has continued to maintain its importance. The original burgh consisted of a small area around the Castlegate, Green and Gallowgate. Expansion through the construction of housing and industrial estates on its periphery – combined with changes in local government boundaries – has increased the area to include once suburban villages such as Bridge of Don, Bucksburn and Dyce in the north, Cove in the south, and Cults and Culter in the west.

Although the traditional industries of shipbuilding, granite working, textile manufacturing, paper-making and fishing have either declined or disappeared, Aberdeen has enjoyed new prosperity as the unofficial offshore oil capital of Europe following the discovery of North Sea oil in 1969. This has brought dramatic changes to the local economy with new job opportunities for both the local workforce and newcomers to the city.

Aberdeen is often referred to as the 'Granite City' or 'Silver City' because its buildings sparkle in the sunshine, although it can look bleak in the wind and rain. Its architectural heritage owes much to the skills of craftsmen who were able to translate the designs created by various notable architects into the buildings still visible on the city's streets today. The granite used came from Rubislaw and various north-east quarries, including Kemnay and Peterhead. The combined skills of architect and granite-worker are displayed not only in the intricate grandeur of Marischal College, Music Hall, the City Art Gallery, Town House and the trio of buildings on Rosemount Viaduct – the City Library, St Mark's Church and His Majesty's Theatre – but also in a range of other buildings.

Aberdeen has long had a reputation as a holiday destination, and outdoor summer entertainment often centred around the beach, where facilities were enjoyed by both visitors and local people. Here families could spend time paddling, enjoying rides on the scenic railway or swimming at the Beach Bathing Station. For the sports enthusiast there were tennis courts and bowling greens, while the Beach Ballroom was advertised in the late 1940s as 'Scotland's finest social centre' when its resident band was Blanche Coleman and her All Girls Band. For those wet and windy days there was His Majesty's Theatre staging plays and musicals, the Tivoli Theatre for variety shows, and the Pavilion where Harry Gordon and his company entertained thousands of Aberdonians and summer visitors over many years. During this period, the city also had a range of cinemas including the Majestic, Queen's and Capitol.

The floral displays in Aberdeen's parks and gardens have earned it the title of 'best city' in the Scotland in Bloom competition on many occasions, while the Winter Gardens in Duthie Park are a major tourist attraction.

The city's motto – *Bon Accord*, meaning 'good fellowship' – is reputed to derive from its use as the watchword during the capture of the Castle of Aberdeen by the army of Robert the Bruce, when it was occupied by English troops under Edward I. It is often used in conjunction with the greeting 'Happy to meet, sorry to part, happy to meet again'.

We hope that these photographs from collections held by Aberdeen Library and Information Services and Aberdeen Art Gallery and Museums will evoke memories of some historical aspects of the City of Aberdeen.

This photograph was taken on Schoolhill where a group of curious onlookers are admiring the work of a pavement artist just outside Aberdeen Art Gallery and Gray's School of Art. The premises that would later be so well-known to Aberdonians as Taylor's Art Salon are just visible on the right bearing the sign Aberdeen Photographic Co. Alexander Taylor set up a photographer's business at 45 Schoolhill in 1892, and over the years the family firm expanded to include picture frame making and artists' materials before it was sold in 1977. It later traded as Sime Malloch Ltd. and is currently Service Point UK, specialising in graphic art and office supplies. The buildings on the right were demolished *c.*1900 to make way for the Central School, which eventually became Aberdeen Academy and has now been redeveloped as the Academy Shopping Centre.

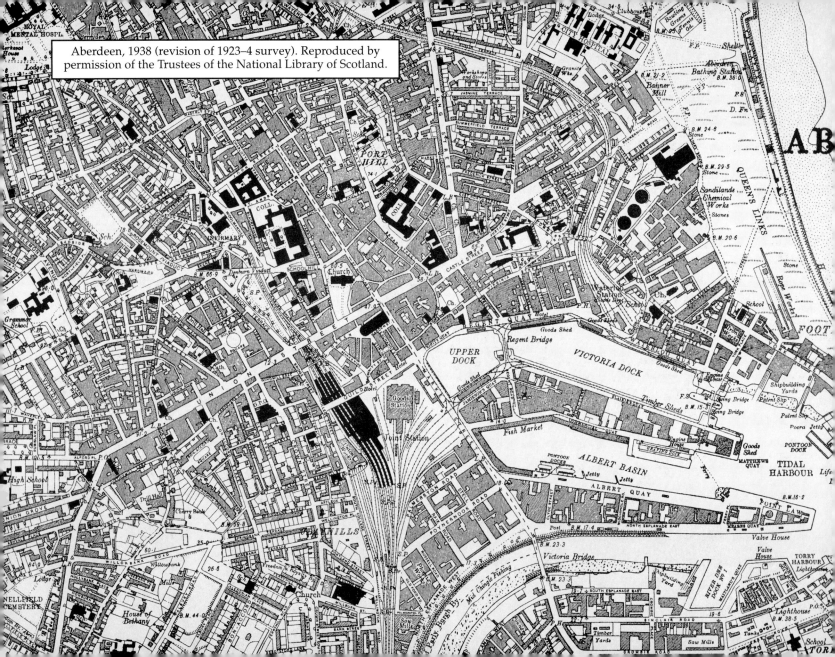

King Street was built at the beginning of the nineteenth century when an Act of Parliament, passed on 4 April 1800, authorised the building of two new streets in the city (the other was Union Street). This view, dating from around 1890, was taken at the junction of Union Street and King Street with the Castlegate leading off to the right. Much of the west (left) side of King Street as seen here is a monument to the work of two notable Aberdeen architects, Archibald Simpson and John Smith. The building in the foreground was designed in 1839 by Simpson for the North of Scotland Bank,

which later became the Clydesdale Bank. It has recently been converted into a bar and restaurant named the Archibald Simpson. A terracotta statue by James Giles, depicting Ceres, the goddess of plenty, surmounts the curved portico with its Corinthian columns. The square tower in the middle distance, with its upper circular section echoing the Temple of the Winds at Athens, belongs to the North (later North and Trinity) Church. This was designed by John Smith in 1829 and converted to form Aberdeen Arts Centre in 1963. The distinctive appearance of the tower gave the church its nickname of the 'Pepperpot Kirk'. Situated in the group of buildings between the kirk and the bank is the Medico–Chirurgical Society Hall, with its Ionic columns, designed by Archibald Simpson in 1818 for the society's meetings and to house their library of medical texts.

The view from the top of the Town House as seen in 1892 differs substantially from that of today, although the spire of the Tolbooth is still visible. Friday's Rag Fair was in full swing in the Castlegate when this photograph was taken, while work was continuing to clear the site at the east end of the square for the building of the Salvation Army Citadel. The old Record Office, which stood at the top of Justice Street, had been demolished in 1891 and the street widened. On the hoarding at the demolition site a notice can just be seen proclaiming the

forthcoming erection of the Citadel and inviting contributions to the building fund. Demolition of the remaining buildings, including the premises of James Watson, cabinetmaker (facing the camera at the end of Castlegate), followed quickly and on 17 August 1893 the foundation stone of the Citadel was laid. It was officially opened on 21 June 1896, effectively obscuring from view the massive structure of the Castlehill Barracks, opened in 1796 as a home for visiting soldiery. The barracks remained the home base of the Gordon Highlanders until 1934 when the regiment moved to their new headquarters at Bridge of Don, after which the Castlehill building was used as flats to ease the housing shortage. All trace of the barracks finally disappeared in the late 1960s with the redevelopment of the Castlehill area and the construction of high-rise blocks of flats.

This *c*.1950 view of the Castlegate looking east to the Salvation Army Citadel captures a city transport system at a time of transition. In the immediate foreground is a streamlined English Electric/Pickering Corporation tram dating from the 1940s. This ran on the bridges route from Bridge of Dee to Bridge of Don. Immediately behind are two older trams of 1927 and 1931, much less modern-looking in their styling, while to their right is a double decker bus. The first Corporation bus came into service in 1920, and from the earliest days buses challenged the dominance of the trams. They didn't require the expensive infrastructure of tramlines and overhead cables, and were much more flexible because their routes weren't fixed. As more cars and lorries appeared on the roads complaints about trams impeding the progress of other traffic increased. The Corporation began to cut back on the maintenance of the tram system and gradually closed routes, replacing them with buses. In May 1958 trams were taken out of service completely, culminating with a spectacular bonfire of them at the city's Queen's Links.

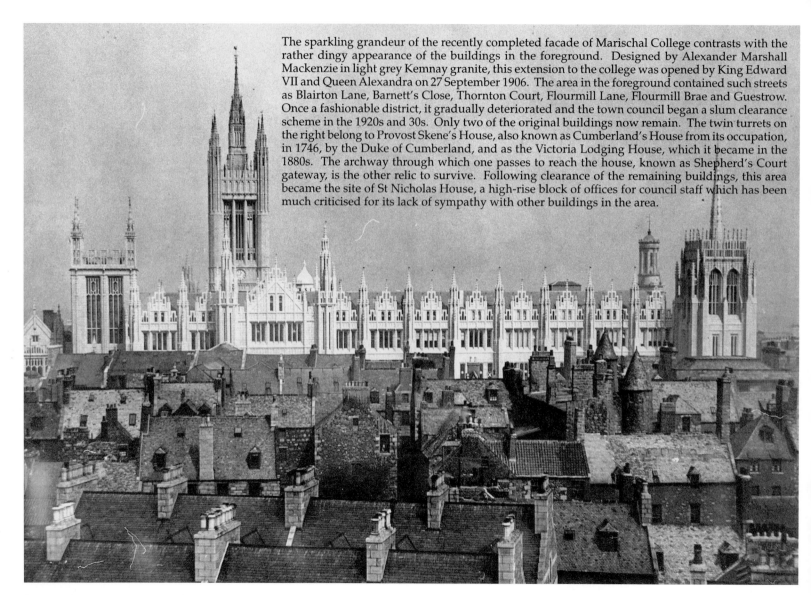

The sparkling grandeur of the recently completed facade of Marischal College contrasts with the rather dingy appearance of the buildings in the foreground. Designed by Alexander Marshall Mackenzie in light grey Kemnay granite, this extension to the college was opened by King Edward VII and Queen Alexandra on 27 September 1906. The area in the foreground contained such streets as Blairton Lane, Barnett's Close, Thornton Court, Flourmill Lane, Flourmill Brae and Guestrow. Once a fashionable district, it gradually deteriorated and the town council began a slum clearance scheme in the 1920s and 30s. Only two of the original buildings now remain. The twin turrets on the right belong to Provost Skene's House, also known as Cumberland's House from its occupation, in 1746, by the Duke of Cumberland, and as the Victoria Lodging House, which it became in the 1880s. The archway through which one passes to reach the house, known as Shepherd's Court gateway, is the other relic to survive. Following clearance of the remaining buildings, this area became the site of St Nicholas House, a high-rise block of offices for council staff which has been much criticised for its lack of sympathy with other buildings in the area.

Guild Street takes its name from Dr William Guild, Principal of King's College in the seventeenth century and one of the foremost Covenanting ministers of the time. Her Majesty's Opera House, on the left of the picture, opened in December 1872 with the play *Lady of Lyons*. The first Christmas pantomime was *Little Goody Two Shoes*, the best seats for which cost three shillings and sixpence. Her Majesty's distinctive appearance derives from the architects' (C. J. Phipps and James Matthews) use of red Peterhead granite, interspersed with bands of white granite and red Turriff sandstone. The arches above the windows are inlaid with white ornamental bricks, while the use of concrete for the side, back and party walls was the first in Scotland on this scale. When His Majesty's Theatre opened on Rosemount Viaduct in 1906, Her Majesty's closed, reopening as the Tivoli in July 1910. Many will remember it in its heyday when the summer variety shows attracted packed houses. The last live show (with Calum Kennedy) was staged in 1966, after which the theatre became a bingo hall until finally closing its doors in 1997. The Tivoli Theatre Trust is now seeking funding to enable the building to be restored to its former glory.

The building of His Majesty's Theatre in 1906 completed the trio of public buildings on Rosemount Viaduct known to Aberdonians as 'Education, Salvation and Damnation'. This photograph, however, predates the theatre and shows the area shortly after the completion of the public library and the South United Free Church in 1892. The imposing South Church (now St Mark's), occupying a commanding site facing Union Terrace and Bridge, was built for one of the largest congregations in the city when its original church in Belmont Street became too small for its needs. A church census revealed a congregation of 1,023 at one particular service. The original library building seen here was extended further west in 1905 to the junction with Skene Street, with the addition of the now familiar tower and dome. In 2003 libraries across the country celebrated 150 years of the Public Libraries Act in Scotland, which came into effect on 20 August 1853. William Wallace appears to be gesturing towards the vacant theatre site but in fact his statue predates all three buildings. Erected in 1888, before the viaduct had been completed, the statue was the gift of John Steill, a lifelong admirer of the Scottish patriot.

This night-time view looking up Union Street was taken in the 1930s and reveals how the street gradually rises towards its western end. In the foreground on the right is Archibald Simpson's North of Scotland Bank building of 1839–42. Beyond, with the tall spire and illuminated clock, is Peddie and Kinnear's Town House (1868–72). The laying out of Union Street was one of the major undertakings of early nineteenth century Aberdeen. Moving from the heart of the town at the Castlegate in the east it passes across the Denburn Valley via Union Bridge. The bridge, designed by Thomas Fletcher with advice from Thomas Telford, was completed in 1805. This was a major feat of civil engineering, but just as difficult was the section from west of the Town House to the Denburn. This required extensive raising of levels with the street running on a number of granite arches.

Cattle being driven across George Street at its junction with Hutcheon Street *c.*1955. This image serves as a reminder that Aberdeen was a market town until the 1980s, with the auction mart located not far away at Kittybrewster. Every Friday many farmers and even more beasts appeared on the streets of the city. Being a market town meant that Aberdeen also provided all kinds of additional services to the farming community, not least a slaughterhouse. This, with associated hide and tallow dealers, was located just behind the Butcher's Arms pub (named after its clientele, and of which Alex McBride was the publican when this photograph was taken). The bar opened *c.*1901 and replaced the Butcher's Tavern. Killing animals and processing hides was a smelly trade and many complaints were voiced about the slaughterhouse. It finally closed in 1974, after which Langstane Housing Association built flats on the site.

This parade of floats and decorated vehicles was probably arranged to mark the coronation of King George VI in 1937. Most prominent in the photograph, taken on Union Bridge, is the Royal National Lifeboat Institution (RNLI) lifeboat. This may be the *Robert and Ellen Robson*, a rowing lifeboat stationed at the beach between 1925 and 1939. At the time of this parade the RNLI was a relative newcomer to Aberdeen, having taken over the city's lifesaving service in 1925. Aberdeen's lifeboat service dates back to 1803 when it was managed by the Aberdeen Shipmaster Society, a local benevolent society. The decision was taken to provide a lifeboat following the disastrous storms of January 1800 when many vessels were lost along the north-east coast. From 1810 the Harbour Commissioners managed a series of lifeboats until the RNLI took over in 1925. The first RNLI rescue took place in September 1927 when the trawler *Ben Torc* went aground at Girdleness. Its crew of six was rescued, including the skipper, still wearing his bowler hat!

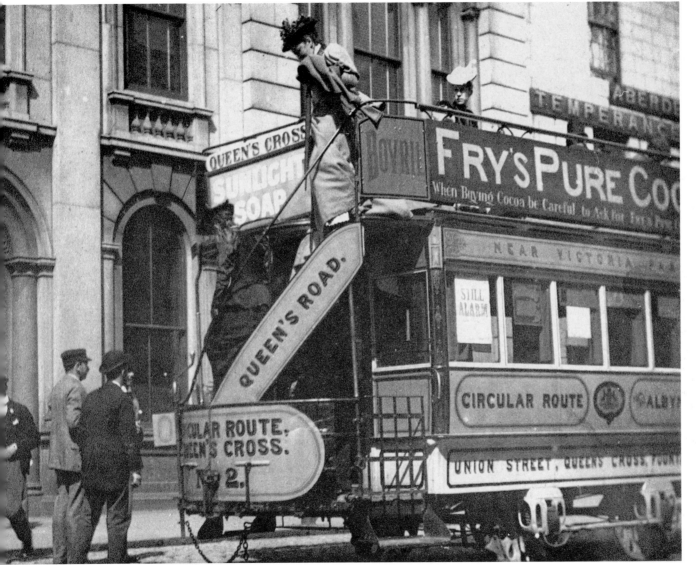

This horse-tram has stopped outside the North of Scotland Bank in Union Street to allow two ladies to descend from its upper deck. It was probably built locally by R. & J. Shinnie, and was painted yellow for the Queen's Cross circular route. The Aberdeen District Tramways Company introduced trams to the city in 1874, with only six cars in operation running on two routes: from Queen's Cross to King Street and from St Nicholas Street to Causewayend. The number of routes and cars increased as the service developed, and in 1898 the tramways company was bought out by the town council, which electrified the service. The last trams ran in the city in 1958, with more than 60,000 people turning out to watch the farewell procession in May. In the early morning of 12 May the remaining cars were burnt at the beach, an event witnessed by only a few people.

The railway yards at Kittybrewster, photographed in 1930. Like many parts of Aberdeen this is an area that has seen many changes over the past three decades. Kittybrewster station and marshalling yard (opened in 1854) originally formed part of the heart of the Great North of Scotland Railway, which sent its trains north and west from here. Following its opening, the company's lines became important economic and social links for villages throughout the north-east of Scotland. Whether it was Kemnay on Donside finding an economical way of transporting granite to Aberdeen, or the small fishing villages on the coast supplying fish to markets in England, the railway was a lifeline. By the time this photograph was taken the GNSR had been absorbed into the London & North Eastern Railway. Today, the only reminder of this once important yard and station is the line to the north, Inverness and beyond.

A pre-First World War Crossley motor car with an Aberdeen 'RS' registration. The photograph was taken *c.*1910 in the garage of Claud Hamilton of Union Street, which proudly advertised itself as a 'works and garage for 100 cars open day and night'. In the early days of motoring, especially in cities, many houses did not have room to garage a car and so businesses such as this one often offered lock-up parking facilities as well as repair services. This probably explains why Claud Hamilton's garage was open day and night. When the photograph was taken motoring was largely the preserve of the wealthy, and in those pioneering days the romance of the internal combustion engine had not been spoiled by congestion and pollution. The advertising signs which adorn the walls of the garage hint at the growing importance of the oil and automobile industries.

The proud Harper family in the 110th motor car to be registered in Aberdeen. It is parked outside Seafield House, the home of John Harper, the man seated in the front smoking a cigar. Directly behind him (with the large beard) is his brother Hugh. These two men were responsible for setting up one of Aberdeen's best-known engineering businesses. They were brought up in Turriff, at the Mill of Laithers, but c.1857, when they were in their twenties, they opened an iron gate and wire manufacturing business in Aberdeen. Their products were to be found throughout the north-east of Scotland as they supplied wire fencing with cast iron posts and iron gates to large estates such as Glentanar and companies such as the Great North of Scotland Railway. From these beginnings the brothers went on to set up their own foundry and machine shops, building suspension bridges and going on to specialise in the manufacture of power transmission systems. John Harper died in 1906 and his brother Hugh in 1912.

A smartly turned-out group of horses and carts photographed on Albert Street in the 1930s. Identification is difficult, but from feint lettering on the side of one of the carts these might have belonged to Kennerty Dairy of Rose Street and Culter. It's not clear why they have assembled for a photograph, but what the picture does reveal is that well into the 1930s horse-drawn vehicles remained an important part of the city scene. This was especially true of dairy business, where horse-drawn transport continued to be used by some firms into the 1950s. The continued reliance upon such vehicles meant there was still a place for the skilled cartwright and wheelwright. Whilst the rapid spread of motor vehicles eventually made many of these firms redundant, some companies, such as J. & J. Ingram of Hutcheon Street, gradually moved from manufacturing carts to motor bodies.

A seven-foot diameter section of cast iron pipe destined for the Girdleness sewerage outfall is pulled along Greyhope Road by a steam traction engine *c*.1902. This major civil engineering project, which required boring through hard granitic rock and under the River Dee, was designed to cope with the increasing volume of domestic and commercial sewage coming from the city. Tunnelling went on 24 hours per day. This section of pipe was for the seaward end of the scheme, just below the lighthouse, and the pipeline was large enough to discharge 81 million gallons of waste directly into the sea daily. Today's regulations would not allow untreated waste to be dumped straight into the sea, but despite this shortcoming the scheme was one of the great civil engineering projects of Victorian/Edwardian Aberdeen. It made the city a cleaner, safer and more sanitary place, and probably had a greater impact on the health of Aberdonians than medical services did at the time. The final cost of the sewerage project was £200,000.

This photograph of members of Aberdeen Fire Brigade was taken in 1875. Until the end of the nineteenth century the brigade was run on a part-time basis. Firemen were paid a retaining fee but continued in their normal jobs, being called out to fires either by the ringing of the Town House bell in daytime, or by being woken up by the town's night-watchmen or policemen at night. Prior to 1885, when the city acquired its first steam horse-drawn fire engine, fires were fought with a manual engine such as the one the men are standing in front of here. About 24 men – twelve on each side – were required to operate the pump, an extremely exhausting task. Until 1887 firemen were only provided with a helmet and belt, and not all of those in the picture have a uniform. In 1896 the fire brigade was put on a more professional footing when firemen became full-time and William Inkster was appointed as the city's firemaster. His predecessor had had to combine running the brigade with his duties as the inspector of lighting. The first purpose-built fire station was opened on King Street on 31 May 1899, and was manned by eleven permanent and ten auxiliary officers, plus the firemaster and deputy firemaster.

Aberdeen has always taken pride in its role as a seaside resort. In this view, Aberdonians and visitors alike enjoy the fine sandy beach and refreshing sea breezes. Bathing coaches were available for hire during the summer months, with the male and female bathing areas strictly segregated. As their use declined in later years the council put the coaches into storage before they were offered for sale in 1953 as mementoes of a bygone bathing era. Situated in a prominent position overlooking the beach is the splendid Beach Bathing Station, with its monumental chimney stack extending 70 feet into the air. Equipped with a large swimming pool, Russo–Turkish baths, private bathrooms for ladies and gentlemen and a large, well-furnished refreshment room, it served its patrons very well. On the right of the picture is the Beach Shelter, which offered a comfortable retreat during inclement weather. It was demolished in 1986, and although the distinctive clock tower on top of the building was saved it was regrettably damaged whilst in storage and ultimately dismantled.

THE BATHING STATION, BEACH, ABERDEEN.

The Beach Bathing Station was designed by city architect John Rust. Its swimming 'pond' opened in July 1898 and at the time was described as the largest in Scotland, measuring 90 by 35 feet and increasing in depth from 3 to 7 feet. It was equipped with 45 dressing boxes for bathers and had a spectators' gallery laid with pitch pine flooring. The pool was situated below ground level so as not to spoil the appearance of the rest of the building. Sea water was pumped in daily and heated to a temperature of 70° F, but by 1958 fresh water was preferred. An expert swimming instructor was always in attendance and lessons were available at a shilling each. The pool was used extensively by generations of Aberdonians, local swimming clubs, military and other organisations, but its gradual deteriorating condition coincided with a declining number of users, leading to its closure in 1972. On Sunday 16 July, as the last swimmer left the pool, the huge outlet valve was opened to allow the water to drain away forever.

This early 1900s photograph shows passengers boarding a horse-drawn bus outside the distinctive red brick structure of the Beach Bathing Station with its covered veranda. From June to September conveyances provided by Campbells (established 1832) left Union Street, near the Queen's statue, at half-hourly intervals for the Links and Bathing Station. In an advertisement in the *Aberdeen Post Office Directory* of 1900, Campbells are described as 'Post Horse Masters to Her Majesty, Omnibus, Carriage and Cab Proprietors'. Their head offices and stables were located in Bon-Accord Street and they had branches in Rosemount and Mounthooly. The company offered 'a splendid selection of thoroughly broken, seasoned and well-bred, stylish carriage horses with beautifully matched pairs in all colours'. Passengers travelling with Campbells could expect to ride in safety and comfort. A later advert of 1914 refers to a '30-h.p. motor char-a-banc for 34 passengers for long-distance runs'. Certainly by the 1930s their cream coaches were touring daily to Braemar, Alford and Edzell, encouraging customers to enjoy the benefits of the open air.

A busy holiday Monday in May 1931 at the beach amusement park. In the foreground some thrilled passengers are enjoying a trip on the scenic railway, erected in 1929 and damaged by fire in December 1940. Other attractions such as the caterpillar, whirlwind and baby motor car track are also visible in the picture. In the left background is the new Beach Pavilion which opened in May 1928 and replaced the original wooden structure with its corrugated iron roof. During the 1920s and 30s the pavilion is best remembered for the summer seasons of Harry Gordon and his Entertainers. A typical programme featured Jack Holden, Gordon Munro, the Pavilion Girls and the pianist Alice Stephenson, who appeared in every summer show with Harry until he gave up the tenancy in 1940. Beyond the pavilion was the Beach Ballroom, with its restaurant and tea lounge. Aberdeen's luxurious new dance hall, with its silky sprung floor accommodating 1,000 dancers, opened in May 1929 in spectacular fashion with a masked ball and carnival. Famous band names to perform there included Joe Loss, Victor Sylvester, Humphrey Lyttleton, and Ivy Benson with her all-girl band.

The abiding memory of the Beach Pavilion is of the summer months between the wars when Harry Gordon was the resident performer. His show was the outstanding feature of the Aberdeen holiday season, and holiday guides always contained adverts promoting it. Harry produced and directed the show himself, even writing the programme and designing its cover. This example dates from 1924.

In 1921 Aberdeen Model Yacht and Power Boat Club sought permission from the town council to use a pond for sailing model yachts. After due consideration, the council agreed that the lower pond in the Duthie Park should be made available on Saturday afternoons for model yachting by the 85-strong membership of the Aberdeen and Torry clubs. Agreement was also reached that the pond should be extended by 30 yards to 150 yards. In July 1930 races were organised for members of the Chums Club of Associated Scottish Newspapers, and competitions were also held for the Reid Cup. The events drew large crowds. The shrubbery and trees in the vicinity of the pond gave rise to requests for their removal because their 'blanketing effect' interfered with the free sailing of their boats, but the pleas of the yacht clubs' members were mostly turned down by the council.

Children and adults relaxing at and in the paddling pond at Westburn Park, *c*.1930. This park, which is situated north-west of the city centre, was opened in 1901 and was one of a number which the council developed in the nineteenth and twentieth centuries. Situated within the grounds is Westburn House, designed by Archibald Simpson in 1839 and at one time the home of the Chalmers family, founders of the *Aberdeen Journal*. The park, with its open grassy areas, tennis courts, bowling greens and pool, is more suited to leisure activities than quiet contemplation. Directly across from Westburn Park is Victoria Park, first proposed in 1871. With its floral displays, shrubs and trees it is a place for sitting on a bench and watching the world go by. The parks movement was a Victorian initiative which sought to bring a hint of countryside to the city and in this way relieve some of the gloom and pressures associated with industry and town living. Parkland was intended to not only enhance physical well-being but also to give a moral and spiritual uplift to visitors.

Two men enjoy a game of draughts at Union Terrace Gardens in the 1930s, a scene which could have been witnessed in the city up to the 1970s. The draughts facilities were run by the city council and gave hours of pleasure to locals, including those who simply looked down on the games from the balustrade on Union Terrace. The gardens, which sit in the hollow of the Denburn valley, were laid out in the 1880s following the building of Rosemount Viaduct and provided the city centre with a quiet, restful spot. Their eastern edge is bounded by the railway, which must have made for some very smoky encounters in the days of steam trains. Over the years there have been a number of attempts to redesign the gardens including a proposal to raise them to street level and provide parking below, but currently they remain pretty much as they did in the 1880s.

A wing walker (possibly Martin Hearn) on an Avro 504K biplane flying over Seaton in the 1930s. This 'barnstorming' spectacle was probably part of Alan Cobham's Aviation Display Day. Cobham's team also used Tiger Moths, Gipsy Moths and Desoutters. This was a time when flight was very much a novelty and still a pioneering way of travelling. At shows such as this spectators were given the opportunity to take short flights, something that would have been viewed with great excitement as few people could afford to travel by air. Commercial aviation came to Aberdeen in the 1930s when for a short while the Seaton site, where this photograph was taken, was used as an aerodrome by E. E. Fresson. But it was Eric Gandar Dower, not Fresson, who successfully developed Dyce Airport, with his company's first flight taking off in September 1934. Dyce had four grass runways, offices and a clubhouse. Under the banner of Aberdeen Airways Gandar Dower established links with Glasgow, Orkney and Shetland. In 1937 he pioneered an air link with Stavanger in Norway but this was not commercially successful.

A 1951 aerial view of the St Clements/Aberdeen Links area. In the nineteenth century a whole cluster of industries developed here, the most prominent of which was the gasworks, seen with its three storage tanks to the left of the main complex. The New Gas Light Company opened its works on the site in 1843, eventually replacing Aberdeen's first gasworks which was at Poynernook. Adjacent to the gasworks is Sandilands Chemical Works. George Miller of Glasgow came to the city in 1848 and leased this site for the processing of 'ammoniac water', a by-product of gas manufacture which he turned into fertiliser. In the foreground is the large timber yard of John Fleming & Co. Fleming established his Aberdeen business in August 1877, but it was only in 1884 that he opened a sawmill in the city, at Albert Quay. In 1903 the company moved to large new premises near the gasworks. At the bottom left of the photograph, nestling amongst the noise and smells of industry, is St Clement's Kirk, built in 1828. During the Disruption of 1843, the minister, Alexander Spence, with most of his congregation, helped form the Free Church of Scotland.

Esparto grass being unloaded by mobile crane from a ship at Aberdeen harbour, *c.*1960. The grass was for use in paper manufacture at one of the north-east's papermills. Esparto grass, *Stipa tenacissima*, is native to North Africa and cultivated in Spain. It is high in fibre and suitable for manufacturing higher quality papers. At one time it was commonly used at Culter Paper Mills and Tait of Inverurie. In the 1950s Culter was using 350 tons of the grass per week, at which time it required two and a half tons of esparto to produce one ton of paper. The grass was boiled in a caustic mixture, washed and bleached and blended with wood pulp to produce the necessary quality. Culter Mills closed in the early 1980s, and since then one further local paper mill, Donside, has also succumbed to competition. On its closure in 2001 some 250 people lost their jobs.

An employee at Aberdeen Comb Works turning horn tumblers *c.*1950. From the 1830s until the 1930s most of this factory's products were made from horn. At its height it was a very large enterprise with about 1,000 workers manufacturing some 25 million combs annually (an average of almost 100 per worker per day). In addition to combs the company also made spoons, snuff boxes and tumblers, all fashioned from horn. Changes in taste and the introduction of new materials forced the company to turn to man-made plastics, the first of

which was a casein based product which had the trade name Keronyx. This was later superseded by cellulose acetate products, the combs going under the name of Nuroid. These were injection moulded rather than cut by machine or by hand. In 1969 a disastrous fire hit the factory but phoenix-like it arose from the ashes and continued trading. However, in 1997 the owners decided to move production from the city.

This view of the interior of the reference department at Aberdeen Central Library was taken in 1930. Andrew Carnegie opened the main library building on Rosemount Viaduct on 5 July 1892, but the reference section was not opened until 29 August. At first, only volumes such as encyclopaedias, atlases and dictionaries were freely available on the shelves, and readers had to complete an application form to gain access to the remaining material. Marble busts including one of Alexander Bain, Professor of Logic at Aberdeen University and supporter of the public library, were on display. The extension to the library allowed more room for reading tables and books on open shelves, and the department was always busy with those seeking information or studying for exams. Over the years the library has been refurbished to remove the very high shelves in the picture and to introduce modern technology in the form of public access computers.

The Girls' Academy was founded in 1874 and occupied premises in Little Belmont Street. Its headmaster was John McBain, who remained in post until 1912, and employed visiting masters for modern languages, singing and elocution. In 1881 the school's name was changed to the High School for Girls, and in 1891 Aberdeen School Board purchased and reconstructed the Female Orphan Asylum, founded by Mrs Mary Elmslie at 19 Albyn Place, to provide larger premises for the growing roll of pupils. This photograph shows the playground at the back of the building at Albyn Place. Despite its name, a limited number of boys between the ages of four and eight were admitted to the preparatory department of the high school until the early 1920s. Over the years a number of extensions have been built and adjacent properties acquired to improve the facilities for the increasing numbers of pupils. In the 1960s primary classes were phased out. A still greater change took place in the 1970s with the introduction of comprehensive education and amalgamation with Ruthrieston Secondary School to form the co-educational Harlaw Academy.

This is Low's Bookstall, a haven for book-lovers in the heart of the city. It was once to be found at Nos. 39–54 on the gallery of Aberdeen's New Market. With the shelves overflowing and stacks of books on the floor there was plenty to keep collectors and readers engrossed. This large covered market, designed by Archibald Simpson, was built in 1840–42. On 29 April 1882, 40 years after it opened, a fire broke out in a basketmaker's store, rapidly taking hold and sweeping through the market, reducing much of it to rubble. Accounts describe the fire as spectacular with the 'sizzling, crackling, and spluttering' of tallow fat coming from the sides of beef hanging in the butchers' stalls. Troops were called in to regulate the crowd. The market was rebuilt and was described as 'one of the sights of the town'. With its butchers, fishmongers, grocers, fruit and vegetable stalls, the lower area was a place of great bustle, while the tranquillity of the bookstall could be found above on the gallery. In 1971 the site was redeveloped, the old market was cleared and a meaner, more claustrophobic space replaced it.

Market day in the Green *c*.1960, an occasion when market gardeners and others brought their wares to the city. The street's name is derived from the access it gave to bleaching and drying greens at the nearby Denburn. With the building of Union Street the north side of the Green saw a radical change. Tall granite buildings (seen on the right of the photograph) went up replacing the smaller dwellings that had stood there beforehand. It seems that at one time it was the pastime of 'certain idle and disorderly persons' standing on high ground to throw 'offensive matter' down into the chimneys of these houses. In 1807 the local magistrates acted and offered a reward of five guineas for the apprehension of these vandals. On the right of the picture, in the background, the magnificent teapot sign which graced the shop frontage of tea merchant John Adams' shop for many years can just be seen. The Green still hosts an open-air market, but sadly it is only a pale reflection of former days.

This 1930s view has a much earlier feel to it, with the forestairs, pantiled roofs and rubble-built walls of the houses providing a stark contrast to the granite tenements that comprise much of the housing stock in central Aberdeen. The location has not been positively identified but it is thought to be the Hardweird–Gilcomston area, in which case these houses would have once formed part of the distinct Denburn community. Shoemakers and weavers were to be found here as well as bleachfields and tanneries. In the 1780s this was referred to as a 'fine village', but by 1818 some of the buildings were described as 'mean and very irregular'. By the twentieth century many of the older properties had become slums with poor if any sanitation, and the council began to place closure orders against them. But the process of closure and clearance was slow and the shortage of housing acute. In the 1930s over 25% of one room dwellings in the area were said to be overcrowded, and in Aberdeen as a whole 10% of accommodation lacked an indoor fresh water supply and acceptable sanitation.

Prefabs at Ashgrove, *c*.1950. This leafy, suburban housing scheme, north of the city centre, was a far cry from the overcrowded housing conditions prevailing in parts of Aberdeen at the time. The houses were a post-war response to the chronic housing shortage, being relatively cheap to build and fast to erect. At the end of World War II pressure for housing was so great that some families squatted in redundant military camps. To ease the pressure and prevent any possible social commotion the government supplied prefabs to local authorities. A prototype was displayed in the Tate Gallery in 1945. Aberdeen was allocated some 1,500 prefabs, which were a revelation to those working class families fortunate enough to be given one. They were completely self-contained and had gardens, a fridge and a bathroom. This was vastly different from standard accommodation in Aberdeen tenements, which by and large had shared toilets and no bathrooms. The temporary houses lasted well beyond their expected life, the last ones being demolished at Tullos in the 1980s.

Salmon fishers at work on the River Dee in the 1930s. Records of salmon fishing on the river date back to the fourteenth century. The three men in this picture are engaged in net and coble fishing, in which one end of the net remains ashore while the vessel lets out the rest of it and does a U-turn on the water, bringing the other end to the shore. The two ends are then gathered and the net drawn in. Aberdeen Harbour Commissioners acquired salmon fishing rights on part of the Dee in 1871, allowing them to develop the harbour without coming into conflict with private individuals who had fishing rights. The Harbour Board continued to carry out commercial salmon fishing on the river into the 1980s. Visible in the background are the premises of Douglas R. Craig, fish curer, on North Esplanade West. Both North and South Esplanade were home to a large number of fish processing firms.

The fish market at Commercial Quay (background) photographed in June 1901. Fish has been sold in Aberdeen since at least the fourteenth century. Parson Gordon wrote in 1661 that there was a daily sale at the 'fish crosse' and fish was often sold in the Castle Street area. In 1742 the council established a fish market on the south side of Shiprow, allowing the catch to be landed nearby. This continued to operate until the 1860s when a temporary market was set up on the west side of South Market Street. As the trawling industry took off in the 1880s there was a need for a market closer to the quays where fish was landed. The Commercial Quay market opened at 6 a.m. on 20 May 1889, with the sale of fish beginning at 8 a.m. It was so successful that a number of extensions were required over the years. Although this photograph was taken less than twenty years after the introduction of trawling to Aberdeen, the majority of vessels visible are already steam-powered, with only a few sail fishing vessels dotted among them.

The steam trawler *Terrier* was built at Aberdeen's Hall Russell shipyard in 1905 (the builder's nameplate is visible on the wheelhouse). *Terrier* had a series of owners, most of them Aberdeen-based, throughout her long career before finally being scrapped around 1955. This photograph was taken *c*.1910 when crew members obviously thought it would be amusing to find as many dogs as possible to illustrate the vessel's name. Trawling was still quite a new industry when this photograph was taken. Aberdeen's first catch of trawled fish, consisting of three boxes of haddock, had been landed in March 1882. The vessel involved was a converted wooden paddle tug, called *Toiler*, brought to Aberdeen by a syndicate of city businessmen. *Toiler* fished off Aberdeen and landed its catch each morning. Although an old vessel and not really suited to trawling, it was successful enough to persuade local owners to commission purpose-built vessels. The first of many Aberdeen-built trawlers, *North Star*, was launched in 1883 by the Duthie yard. By 1905, the year *Terrier* was built, there were 178 trawlers registered at Aberdeen.

Trawlers undergoing maintenance in Aberdeen's graving dock, *c*.1910. The dock, built in 1885, did not have a long life. Although made of granite it had concrete ends and a concrete bottom, and the salt water caused the concrete to deteriorate. As a result the dock leaked badly, leading to its removal in 1925 after a long period of disuse. The vessels visible in the photograph are: A736 *Kate*, built in 1893, belonging to John Lewis; A782 *Craigievar*, built in 1896, belonging to the Aberdeen Steam Trawling & Fishing Co.; and what appears to be A780 *Craigellachie*, built in 1896 and owned by the Craigellachie Steam Fishing Co. The fourth vessel is unidentified. The introduction of trawling in the late nineteenth century meant orders for the Aberdeen shipyards: 267 vessels were built in the twenty years from 1883. By the early twentieth century Aberdeen was Scotland's largest fishing port, with around 1,000 people employed in trawling. Line fishermen were less happy about the flourishing industry, fearing that fish stocks would be exhausted. However, the boom continued and Thomas Walker, the line fishermen's spokesman, decided to give the new method a try, going on to become one of Aberdeen's most successful trawler owners.

Mrs Gove and Mrs Wood shell mussels and bait fishing lines in Old Torry in the 1920s. Until the late nineteenth century, many men from villages around Aberdeen went small line fishing in undecked boats. The lines, used to catch haddock and cod, were baited with mussels and laid in flat baskets known as sculls. This work was done at home by women, who also gutted the fish and carried it to market. Lines for haddock could have as many as 1,000 hooks. With the advent of bigger boats suitable for trawling and great line fishing many villagers moved to towns with deep-water harbours and small line fishing became less common. By the 1920s, many Torry residents had adopted the new techniques, although others still pursued small line fishing from yawls berthed at Torry harbour. The mussels used as bait were generally collected by women and children, with the Bay of Nigg a popular place for this search.

A 1905 launch at the John Duthie shipyard in Torry. The original Duthie yard, established at Footdee in 1817, was a well-known builder of sailing ships, although from the 1880s its main output was steam trawlers. In 1903 a family dispute led to the establishment of a rival Duthie yard, based across the harbour in Torry. The new enterprise quickly established a good reputation and probably hastened the demise of the older yard, which closed in 1907. This picture shows the launch of *Ballochbuie* for the Aberdeen Lime Company. On the platform in the centre a well-dressed lady, probably connected with the company, can be seen performing the vessel's christening. The Aberdeen Lime Co. was established in 1854 and had premises on Blaikies Quay. It originally owned a fleet of sailing vessels but bought its first steamship in 1882. *Ballochbuie* was another innovation as the vessel was self-trimming. This meant coal could be loaded evenly without the assistance of labourers. Duthie was probably selected as the builder because of the yard's reputation for modern equipment and practices. Unfortunately *Ballochbuie* had a short career, being torpedoed and sunk on 20 April 1917 in the Firth of Forth with the loss of three lives.

Artificially dried salt fish at Williamson & Co.'s Esplanade Curing Works *c.*1920. The firm, which had premises at North Esplanade East close to the Victoria Bridge, had been founded in Shetland in 1899 and established its Aberdeen base in 1904. An advertisement of 1911 states that specialities included sun-dried salt fish, smoked haddock and salted herring. Williamson carried out the sun-drying of salt fish at Balnagask on what is now the golf course. Drying fish such as cod, haddock and ling using the sun was a traditional method, and many people thought that it tasted better than fish dried in kilns. A kiln was expensive to operate but did have advantages: the drying process was much quicker (taking 48 hours rather than two weeks) and work could be done at night and in winter. Most of Williamson's output was for export, with markets in Spain, Portugal, Africa and South America. It remained a family-run business until its sale to the Claben group in 1958.

The fish-curing firm of Allan & Dey was founded in 1892, and when this photograph of the Finnan kiln was taken in 1911 the company employed 250 people, 200 of whom were women. It also took on seasonal staff. While some fish was sold fresh, much was dried or cured. The Finnan Haddie, a haddock that has been split, pickled and smoked over peats, was one variety. Another, close fish or smokies, was haddock (without its head but otherwise whole) smoked over a fire. Allan & Dey also produced fillets, with fish such as cod, saithe and haddock popular. The company seems to have become successful very quickly. A report in 1907 observed that 'as the energy and enterprise of the partners is unbounded, they may be expected in course of time to girdle the rest of the globe with their fish boxes . . . their Finnan Haddies are now much appreciated as breakfast-table luxuries in Egypt, South Africa and Australia' (*Aberdeen Today*, 1907). Allan & Dey's business has changed considerably over the years, and in 1999 it moved its operations out of Aberdeen. Latterly it employed around 40 people, most of them male, and its main products were salmon and monkfish.

Workers at the Aberdeen Fish Manure & Oil Company Ltd., photographed *c.*1920. The factory opened at Cove Bay, just south of Aberdeen, in 1896 and had its own railway siding. A special train brought daily supplies of offal from the fish market and carried away the finished products. As the name suggests the company produced manure and oil from fish. Trimmings were placed in steam dryers to make manure while oil was produced by pressing and boiling fish livers. Demand was so great that the factory operated day and night, stopping only on a Sunday. The customers for fish manure were varied and widespread and manure from the factory went to hop fields in Kent, French vineyards and German beetroot farms. The liver oil was mainly used for lubrication. In 1904 the company employed 25 men, although there are almost 40 in this photograph. However, business seems to have declined in the 1930s and the factory closed around 1938.

Two deckhands from the steam drifter *Primevere* photographed at Aberdeen harbour on 2 May 1956. *Primevere* was built at John Duthie's Torry yard in 1914 for T. E. Thirtle of Lowestoft, and had a number of Lowestoft owners throughout her career. Duthie's Torry shipyard operated from 1903 until 1925 and almost all of its output was steel fishing vessels. Many of these, such as *Primevere*, had lengthy working lives. The Duthie yard did not supply engines, however, and *Primevere*'s came from Elliot & Garrood of Lowestoft. In the background is a John Lewis lorry delivering coal to an adjacent vessel. The John Lewis shipyard was based at Torry but the company also had a separate coal business. When this photograph was taken most of the vessels landing fish at Aberdeen would have been trawlers and great liners. The number of drifters declined greatly during the 1930s due to increased operating costs and a reduced demand for herring.

The Aberdeen Coal Company (which became the Aberdeen Coal & Shipping Company in 1920) was founded in 1900. Coal for the city's fishing fleet was conveyed from the north of England to Aberdeen by chartered ships because of its particular suitability for steam. In 1901 the Aberdeen Coal Company had the *Redhall* built for this trade, followed by other vessels including the *Frederick Snowdon* (lost with all her crew in January 1912) and the *Ferryhill*. Discharging coal at Aberdeen initially involved the use of iron buckets and required up to 70 men to unload a 1,000-ton cargo. Around fifteen to twenty horses and carts would need to be on hand to transport the coal to the trawlers that required it. By 1929 a number of mechanical grabs, which could lift up to two tons at a time, had been introduced, thus speeding up the procedure and also reducing the manpower needed. Increasingly, coal began to be carried by rail, and as steam trawlers gave way to diesel boats so the demand for coal vessels slumped. This picture appears to show pre-bagged coal being weighed and loaded onto a horse-drawn dray.

A 1906 Aberdeen Coal Company letterhead.

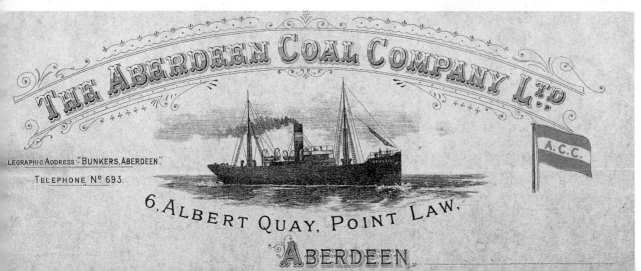

THE ABERDEEN COAL COMPANY LTD.

TELEGRAPHIC ADDRESS: "BUNKERS, ABERDEEN."

TELEPHONE No 693.

A.C.C.

6, ALBERT QUAY, POINT LAW,

ABERDEEN.

Two steam trawlers load bunker coal at Point Law. This coaling facility opened in 1948 on the site of the current Point Law oil terminal and closed again in 1962, by which time there were few coal-burning vessels left. Aberdeen's last coal-powered trawler, *Mount Keen*, was sold for scrap in 1963. The two vessels in this view are *Viking Star* and *Viking Honour*, both belonging to George Robb & Sons Ltd. The photograph dates from the mid-1950s when Robb owned fourteen vessels with the 'Viking' prefix. All of these were quite elderly, the newest being *Viking Consort*, built at Hall Russell in 1924 as *Strathgarry*. *Viking Star* (ex-*Star of Scotland*, ex-*William Beaumont*) was built at Hall Russell in 1918 while *Viking Honour* (ex-*Heugh*) was built at Alexander Hall in 1914. Both were scrapped in 1960. The vessel visible in the background with the white superstructure is *St Ninian* (II), owned by the North of Scotland & Orkney & Shetland Shipping Company. She is probably berthed at the company's old site on Matthews Quay.

The Aberdeen steam trawler *George Robb* passes the harbour's pontoon dock. Built in 1930 for Newhaven owners and originally named *Elise I Carnie*, George Robb & Sons Ltd. bought and renamed her in 1936. She served as a minesweeper during World War II, returning to Aberdeen in 1946. In 1959 she was converted to diesel, but on only her second trip afterwards was wrecked at the Stacks of Duncansby. All twelve crew were lost. *Elise I Carnie* was one of nine steam trawlers built at Hall Russell in 1930. By this time, trawling was well-established with over 300 trawlers registered at Aberdeen. Related businesses also flourished. In 1939 Aberdeen had three fish meal factories (where trimmings such as heads and bones were turned into animal feed), three ice factories, eleven box factories and a range of net-makers and ships' stores. Following World War II the fishing fleet began to modernise. Aberdeen's first diesel trawler, *Star of Scotland*, entered service in 1947. This modernisation process took some time, although *George Robb* was one of only a few remaining steam trawlers when she was converted to diesel in 1959.

This night-time view from the 1930s looks across the Victoria and Upper Docks towards the harbour buildings, with the spire of the Town House visible on the skyline. In the centre of the picture, just behind the steamship, is Regent Bridge, a prominent harbour feature for many years. This bridge, which separated the Upper and Victoria Docks, was opened in December 1904. It replaced a hand-operated drawbridge, installed when the wet dock system was completed in 1850. The new Regent Bridge was a steel swing bridge operated by hydraulic power and carrying two railway tracks, two lanes of road traffic and two footpaths. The railway lines are visible in the foreground of the picture. Work to replace Regent Bridge also provided an opportunity to widen the passage between the two docks to 67 feet, as shipping using the port had increased in size since they were built. The bridge was removed in the 1970s, together with the dock gates, when Aberdeen harbour was redeveloped to provide 24 hour access for North Sea oil industry shipping.

This 1975 photograph shows Aberdeen harbour at a time of major change. The Albert Basin had been the base for the fishing fleet since the 1880s and the dock is busy with trawlers in this view. However, the stern of an offshore supply vessel is also visible on the right, signalling the arrival of the oil industry. The first major oil find was the *Forties* field in 1970. As other discoveries followed, and unusual vessels such as drillships became regular visitors to Aberdeen, it was apparent that the industry was going to be around for several years to come. The harbour required major work to make it suitable for the oil industry: quays were reconstructed and the dock gates removed to allow 24 hour access. There were also changes to the cityscape: the building under construction in the centre of this view is the Salvesen Tower, one of many office blocks built to house the influx of new businesses. Oil also had an impact on Aberdeen's fishing fleet. The industry was going through a difficult period and many owners chose to convert their trawlers to offshore standby vessels.